The Meaning of Flight

To Alan —
Remembering Israel
in March 2007
My best — cojion gosaur,
Chris M.

Also by Christopher Meredith

Poetry
This
Snaring Heaven

Novels
Shifts
Griffri
Sidereal Time

Non-fiction
Cefn Golau: Shooting a Novelist

For children
Nadolig Bob Dydd

Translation
Melog by Mihangel Morgan

The Meaning of Flight

Christopher Meredith

seren

Seren is the book imprint of
Poetry Wales Press Ltd
Nolton Street, Bridgend, Wales, CF31 3BN
www.seren-books.com

ISBN 1-85411-386-0

A CIP record for this title is available from the British Library.

The publisher acknowledges the financial assistance
of the Welsh Books Council.

Printed by Bell & Bain Ltd, Glasgow

Cover photograph: photolibrary.com/OSF/David Fleetham

Contents

What flight meant

I held the art of dying
in my hand today.
Her hurt wings folded in my loose fist
yielding as the fingers of a glove –
a swallow that dipped quick
trawling insects in the lane
clouted by some windscreen out of air
and thud,
distilled into precision.

What flight meant
was the pulsing line of gorging and delight
that drew the smooth blur
of her x on air.

But look. All's gone hard edge.
Swallows are taut arrangements
of black pins and scimitars.
Tailfins, wingtips and the tiny beak
are stanleyknifed to pinpoints.

The swooping black dart of her back
's been startled off by stillness,
fixed different
in these thumbsized shoulders
of intenser poison blue.

The forehead's no black smudge
nor red either, quite,
but minute scumblings of rust.

Those legs that weren't there when she flew
are clean black needles now
as there as sculpture,
and her claws
machines designed to clutch at straws.

When the world's smacked loose from meaning
all's knocked to fuss and artifice and pattern.
Your dying relatives in their beds
see your dentistry, the stitching on your shirt,
contemplate the thereness of their fingertips.

And her. Her eyes are big as black pinheads
clinical as an artist's
amazed this suddenly to see the world,
its mad particularity
so sharp and quick with colour,
so stopped.

The island hours

Snorkel

Early. The gods enter above, masked.
Over their shoulders they drag in sky
and hang crucified or fly
above their shadows cast
over rippled wires of light
that shift with the liquid prism of sea.

The knead and surge work them
to the ruined tiers of a cliff
where bream and snapper drift
rapt in the plotless commerce of another day.

And one god lifts his fins and falls
to feel the lower squeeze and chill
where bars of light blur off to cloudy green
and out of the dark
a shoal of radioactive knives
cuts through his ghost.
Pin-eyes of cinnabar shift in unison.
They have the latest thing in see-through guts.

Far down and darkly
tiger things switch restless tails
staring into encrusted porticos.
The jewellery of citizens gleams
and under him mad wrasse display
the witchoil brilliants in their coats of mail.

Down here the skin's an organ like the eye.
He feels closenesses and colours
as it roughens, soothes
with every swell and rub
and a thrill too close to horror
sends him back up to the sky.
People ashore see a spurt of silver
and he breathes.

But the gods are equipped
with curiosity and harpoon-guns.
And look. One points to the bed.
a flash of spineless flesh
whiter than themselves
gathering its billows of suckered lace
under a shelf of rock.
It gives this squirt of ink, exits.

Slicks

On the parched rocks
your bare legs bleed
in the exhausted scramble
down the thornclogged scree

till at the riven edge
where crowns of mountaineering larch
claw your shins, you stop
and cliffs whiter than thirst

plunge a kilometre to the sea.
Your gasp evaporates
before the air can stir.
Ocean sighs like a tired lung.

Heat gleams. The back of your shirt's
a mane of sweat.
Far down the scalloped shore's
enamelled blue and green.

Seacaves, beachless bays
explain so many fancy words
– *turquoise, azure, cerulean,*
the pun in *ultramarine.*

At first the long blur out at sea
that gleams dull when the lung
swells full seems part of it
but it's greasy, out of focus

as if the sea is drugged.
Another and another daub.
The filmy spectra drift
somewhere between the world and thought.

You try to blink them off and can't,
these dragged-out dirty-rainbow
fingerprints, smears
of sunoil on the eye.

Magic hour

This was the one with the big guns
– jetskis, speedboats, ranks of sunbeds –
the whole bit. But we got there late,
when all the beach had taken home their burns
to salve. Then, Look, she said

and by her brown foot on the lapline
the tiny capsized loggerhead
was paddling air.
The legs or fins or wings, whatever they were,
revolved in absurd syncopations.

One delicate flip of a finger
and he treddled off
the wrong way up the beach.
One skewed heelmark deep as a matchbox
and he turned turtle once again,
struck up another rag.

Filmmakers call this magic hour,
the sun just gone
the light still good enough
to get the shot.

Still my throwaway camera
paused, not for the gloom that would lose
the working on the figured shell
but because sometimes I can understand
the faiths that make no images of god.

Yet snap I did,
after I'd flipped him like a coin
to take his chance.

And the divine comedy
charlie chaplinned down the strand
to hurl himself heroic in the Med.

And they were wings
after all, as he birded through warm sea
and he was Daedalus
we hoped, and not the other one.

Last light slipped away to dusk.
We stood among the regiment of beds,
the outboards cocked and ready
for the morning's first assault.

Night

Siesta done the blinds roll up
from Saint Pavlos to the Markos Square

and in the grottoes of the long arcades
shops blossom like anemones.

Jewellers sit in marble lairs
and watch their bright displays

sugared with diamonds, soothed with lapis lazuli
buttered thick with soft Greek gold.

The phosphorescent glaze on pots
the manikins in neon bras and pants

draw shoals to airconditioned screens
and the embroidered tablecloths, the squares of lace

unfold their complicated traps
exhaling a whiff of naphthalene.

The turning earth takes down the lights a touch.
Night. Eaters gather in the square.

In the darkest corner they've clamped a poet
under stone, his verses trapped in glass

and where they burned their nobles into ash
we crowd tables, order. Waiters rattle out

parakalo with voices dry as night
harvesting strictly democratic cash.

Two girls on a motorbike
each thinner than the island cats

are grooming to be twins,
each body sheathed in a slick of black

each head a strike of steelblonde hair.
They pause and practise looking blank.

In unison the tanned masks scan the square.
The sullen chic finds nothing to its taste.

The first one, or the second, guns the gas.
There's a squirt of poison and they're gone.

Colour

Hot days you'd take a kitchen chair
to the railings where the nettles grew,
and across a summer mile of valleybed
shaleblack and green and lit with the glittering river
you'd watch the far sporadic traffic crawl.

You'd take the shiny spoon and turn
your slurried trifle in the dish
its sugarwet mess the gaudy palette
of incomprehensible childhoods
before we all were born
a war and a strike and another war ago
when Armageddon stood at the turn of the hill
in Troedrhiwgwair.

And under my hand this photograph's a lie –
you simplified in monochrome,
the pinny and the big forearms
grotesque as some comedian in drag,
hands stiffened to arthritic paddles,
two shadows masking pale blue eyes.

A long way off above Man Moel
hanggliders turn in the thermals
the tiny gashes of their bright flags
signalling *we live, we live.*

Sheep on the estate

At night tucked in we listened to the calls.

Pasture roughsquared into gardens,
warm tarmac and the lee of houses,
tippable bins, the spill of ash and scraps
tempted the small diaspora,
their timid insistent pillaging.

We wanted sleep,
told them uselessly to hush
but it was a radio you couldn't stop
tuned somewhere strange-familiar.
The theme was hunger and estrangement.
You could follow the drama's argument
in cross-purpose conversations of the lost.

There was the deep and asking on a rising note

Are you there?

answered distant
in the panic of another's child

Yes, it's me

and another

Yes, it's me.

Then more mothers belled

You? Is it you? Babe? Babe?

And we understood
how each square of tussocks and the nuzzled ash
penned someone in the dark alone.

Yes, it's me.

No, me.

Me.

Gorse country

Where they live
is gorse country.
A scrappy patch of upland
too steep for use
three hundred yards from the bungalows
across a hayfield and a rusted fence
– therefore remote,
thorny, almost safe.

I often walk its lower edge,
sense the community surviving furtively,
see, sometimes, a wing, a scut,
hear, above the distant roar
a whirr and flap.
Summers in the cambered interior
manhattans of foxglove cluster.
Blackbirds rustle curtains.
Slugs ooze out of bars onto dazed streets.
Up there,
bees copter through the sunlit stacks.

*

The trunk of an immense dead elm
flensed white, immaculate as bone
was laid across the hill
a fallen border tower
between the field and this.

Now it's unjointed into discs
a toppled stack of coins
each thicker than my hand can span.
Somebody comes each day when I'm not there.
I watch the progress of unseen dismemberment.
Great steaks of tree
dark ghosts of heartwood for the severed spine,
then tumbled blocks and sawdust fine as ash.

There are places where it's hard to tell
the tracks of beetles from the chainsaw scars.

*

And though the big machines
have harrowed earth in patterns
like a fingerprint
still I come, feed nervously
as its birds do on our lawns.

The field's earmarked.
A close of houses, the sort I might exist in,
gnawing at the borderland, squeezing the space
around the places where I almost feel at peace
and cannot live.

Orang-utan

A radio sings. Too loud.
The children shout. Us.

In the old man's play no radio sings
no children shout. After long stillness
he shuffles in his ragged gown upstage.
And the graceful falling, decorous heap,
each knotty, hennaed rag disposed with art
fanned and folded as on a draped urn.
Behind the folds head vanishes floorward.
Right hand extends across the strawy stage.
The left goes upward. He doesn't look
but from old knowing fingers lock
the intersection of a crucifix
among the bars.
And still.
The tableau is assembled.
He is perfectly composed. The ropes sway.
Leaves on his dying branches flicker once
and sunlight hardening after cloud
casts a lattice over him.
Technique's precise, disciplined as *noh*,
true and unreal
classical acting at its most exact.
Huge emptiness will not be broken
by the stirring of a hair or rib.

While elsewhere his usurping brother's
busy with a chainsaw, he, undaughtered,
without crown or book or staff or all the
places where he was himself, holds the stage.
In the old man's play no radio sings.
No children shout. We are the fourth wall.

Eating an orange

My thumb, penetrating
the budded tips of segments
I vacuum-lipped stray blebs of juice
from the inner skins

unrolled them, moons of fruit
flesh-hinged, in two camps ranged.
Their backs made velvet bulbs
in my cupped hands

and loaded in each venous chamber
like bullets in a flesh revolver
were hard seeds
waiting for the tongue on vulva.

Red armchair

I like to sit in my red armchair
that's rumpled in the morning sun.
I love the bashedup faded warm
of her scuffy terracotta arms
the foursquare squat untippable
strong give of her
the vivid brickred tongue
of her squashed squab
under my lazy arse.
Her fat red cushions are the daily press
that speak of falls and squeezes and slumps.
I throw myself into her
like I've never done with any job
and realize a little late
that the others – the bentwoods, the swivellers,
the ones that claimed to be adjustable,
the tubular sprung steel Bauhaus numbers,
the leggy backless types I've rubbed against
in midnight bars – they all mean nothing
come sober morning in the sun
to this my love, my bearer, my vocation.
She never trod a catwalk or did cool
has not declined from chic to dowdy churl,
was always strong and squashed and firm and giving
and fat with adjectives and never gave a shit
and never so cheap as to yield
to any of my metaphors
but always was is just my red armchair.

Transitory

not another chance for two hundred and forty three years

In the slot of white
from the drawn curtains
I shouldered the waggling
backtofront field glasses.
The blank page waited
with its strip of light.

And my angling turned
to a sort of dance
trouttickling sunlight
out of the skyriver
panning out its nugget
with a dithyrambic swish
and it rolled out of reach
till I teased it to the rim,
milked it out, and it spiralled
in the funnel and spilled
and there my star
bazookaed onto paper
and distilled
minted on the strip,
the silverpale half a crown
of wrong way round sun.

I steadied the dancing
to a mere quiver
and Venus like a beauty spot
a hole punched in an amulet
to hang it at your heart
at your heart
came clear
slipping closer to the limb.

And that day, O my darling,
eighth of June oh-four,
I knew was the last
I would ever see of her.

Cân

Where are you going? the driver said.
I hauled in my bag and I pulled shut the door.

I glywed yr adar sy'n canu i'r wawr.

And where are you going? the driver said.
You young can travel as far as you dare.

I fwydo'r mân adar ar lawntiau'r bore.

And where are you going, the driver said,
in afternoon hills and a lover to lie with?

At lygad goleuni i glywed yr hedydd.

And where are you going, the driver said,
as Venus glows white and the stars start to breed?

I goeden y fwyalch sy'n canu i'r machlud.

And see where you're going, the driver said.
I looked in the glass and a ghost looked at me.

I berfedd tywyllwch, at gân eos ddu.

Famous Czech poet in Dinbych y Pysgod

The menu, sir.

Too much freedom,
the poet says.

Turkey,
lamb,
plaice…

Plaice?

Plaice.

I'll have plaice.
I like fish,
the poet says.

He talks of fish.
For instance,
monkfish.
Nicely cartilaginous
and soft.

He talks of home.
It will be hard.
Too much freedom,
the poet says.

The knife and fork slow
twisting meatless sheets of scales,
albino six inch nails of bone.

There's more on this plate than when I began,
the poet says.

He starts to gag.

Application to the Arts Council
for a grant to write this poem

Sir/Madam
The poem (hereinafter called The Poem)
will consist of approximately 35-45 lines.
In the opening two or three lines
a startling image will be broached.
All nouns at this stage will be concrete
and multisyllabic latinate words
will be avoided.
The immediacy this generates
may well pull the reader (hereinafter
The Reader) through The Poem
with a sense of its integrity,
though it may not necessarily be comprehensible.
This will be facilitated by a firm but
unobtrusive control of rhythm and line
breaks.
More images will follow.
They will establish an atmosphere, a milieu
both oblique and bleak,
perhaps outdoors: a Landscape, some Weather.
Some small detail will suggest the larger world
(e.g., a thumbnail scraping at dried paint
standing for the crisis of lost meaning etc.).
Point of view will be crucial to The Poem.
Late on and subtly it will emerge
That there is an I
about whom (or who) The Reader must be
cautious. (I may not be the author, etc.)
Near the end there will be a shift –
perhaps there is a sudden change of tense.
Earlier images recur, perhaps a little altered,
(e.g. the sky is dark, a thumbnail picks at dried blood)
reflecting and refracting all that has been said.

Your fund provides an excellent opportunity
to embark on The Poem. I have approached
my employers, who are sympathetic, for release.
I believe you favour most those projects
devoted to capital investment.
This is one such. If successful, I plan
to build a house for all eternity.
(My CV is enclosed.)

The Message

....no secrets which appeared to require concealment were revealed.
– Anthony Storr, *Solitude*

She hid her notebooks underneath a board.
All her secret years were what she'd written
And the message – oh the message was in code.

The Lonely Child, Creative, Bright, Ignored
Kept diaries according to the pattern
And hid her notebooks underneath a board.

Years later, experts come upon the hoard
– Keys to the great writer's motivation –
But the message, ah, the message is in code.

They clap their hands. So much to be explored
Deciphering the secret heart of a woman
Who hid her notebooks underneath a board.

And that unlocking lets light on what's stored –
Eventless commonplaces. An empty room. The burden
Is no message is the message in the code.

She knows the cipher's greater than the word.
What's on display's the fact that all is hidden
So she hides her notebooks underneath a board
And the message is the message is in code.

Life of the Poet (index)

birth;
childhood;
schooling;
reading;
early writing;
bullied;
gains entrance
to university;
Lydia:
courtship of,
spurned by,
shyness;
early articles:
rejection of,
his worst,
life at university;
rowing;
takes laudanum;
Christianity:
has doubts about,
courtship of Anne;
burns papers;
prepares for Civil Service;
writing;
swimming;
notebooks;
becomes imitative;
marriage;
finances;
habits and temperament;
Hempelman:
infatuation for,
walking-tour with,
spurned by,
fatherhood and children;
debt;
reviewing;
homes;

Lifefugue of sexual tension in bookshops

If the unnazis came to bookshops
if they came to the bookshops where
the tingling statues were
they'd take books from the shelves
and pick and unpeel the gummed endpapers
peel them back and pull the outers off
flay cookery and gardening
undress the lexicons and travelogues
and in the tense
in the tense shelved bookshop air
in the tense still longing of the statues
in the tense still longing of the people
us in the bookshops
in the radioactive quiet of the hardpressed
tightshut millions of words
in that shut energy
they'd slither bookskins up shins and thighs
unslough buttocks and backs
resheathe shoulders and heads with nudity
unslice the knife along rejoining flesh
until the entire turnedon aching world
was standing naked in a bookshop
blurbed hot with praises
openable to wonderful passages
titles bristling and seriffed
delicate fonts gone wet and yielding
and then the unnazis would uncase
they would uncase the violins
and dancing a little
slide their bows
until the taut air sang
the volume and the mass of us
and every folio and runninghead and colophon
juddered and blurred with forced vibration
until the faint harmonics of our longing

gathered and sang clear
that unbearable inaudible illegible
selftranscription of all keyboards
sang clear the shelves and books
the tingle statues fiddles people dancing
and regathered on that kristallmorgen
revitrified all there was
to a globe a shut unshattered brandybubble
one wordless ringing perfect sphere of glass

The solitary reaper

See him trekking up the hill,
Yon solitary English gent.
He stood a moment as I worked,
Heard me sing a while, and went.
I saw him scribble in a book
Pausing now and then to look
While I cut and bound the crop,
And though I saw, I didn't stop.

I had the whole ridge left to scythe –
anyway, he had a big nose and buck teeth.
Break off and you invite a chat,
and you know how these gentlemen are.
They think the world has two languages –
English and the barking of dogs.
They translate themselves by shouting.
Who wants that?
So I wore my song like armour
to dazzle him.
Still he stopped, and watched, and listened.

And I saw then all that will be.
A million bignosed Englishmen
tumbling in frockcoats down the ridge
equipped with notebooks and sensitivities
and butterfly nets and killing jars.
They watched god fade in cooling sunsets
and wondered about Nature,
talked cosmology and architraves
while miles away ships filled with slaves
and earth stained red.
They wore old jeans
when they made the fourwheeled drive
to the cottage they restored.

In a dream once, one, bucktoothed, came to me
and said See. I also sing
so I'm a native too.
And I turned chill.
His eyes were soft with sentimental anthropology.
I saw my thirteen unborn children dead
and my dugs like satchels in my lap,
the croft stove in and leaking smoke,
the black masts pointing towards Canada.
And all this bloomed the dazzle of my song
and he turned away.

My mother missed the beautiful and doomed

My mother missed the beautiful and doomed
by a few years.
Where Waugh, hot for some pious ormolu,
dreamed Brideshead
she swept carpets, cleaned grates.

Sepia expects a tear
but none comes. She holds
the yellowed postcard of the House
at arm's length, beyond her two dead children,
two atom bombs ago.

'It was like that film. You know. *Rebecca*.'
She smokes.
Echo of casual elegance in the wrist, the gesture,
masks slow scorching of the fuse.
The drag of air
accelerates a hundred small ignitions.
'The drive and all. They had a maze.'
Ash hardens into brightness
small flames eat the paper
worming back along tobacco galleries.
She frowns and jewels, salvers, gleam the harder.
'Her Ladyship 'ould doll up to the nines
come dinner, like a filmstar.'
The mind drags air through fifty years of fading
burns off the filmdream, comes to other stuff,
makes it glow again.

Through half open doors
down perspectives of the glassy rooms
she hears them.
Iw. Mmn. Yiss. Tongues all twangs and daggers.
The Foreign Secretary stands in the hall
his collar of vermiculated astrakhan
flawed with sparkling rain.

She kneels by the scuttle with
an egg of coal in either hand.
His chauffeur in doublebreasted rig
loiters, one glove removed, ruffles her hair,
sets her neat white cap awry.
'Little Cinderella' he says.

She frowns to brighten memory's fuse,
looks down the maze of galleries where
her people cut the coal.
The hand had rained a blow or a flirtation,
the words half flattered her
and kept her down.

She glances sideways at the tight black boot,
the echo of the bentarmed cross.
Krupp's bombs rain now on undefended children
glimmer through smoking Barcelona.

Unwilled complicity can hurt so much.
She clutches at the deaths of millions.

'A skivvy all my life' she says
and strikes another match.

Homecoming

Normally it was sweets.
Fruit Pastilles that I didn't much like
though I couldn't tell him that.
Laying his grub box on the windowsill
tugging the buckle of his raincoat loose
he'd reach them down to where I read my comic.
I'd take them without looking up.

But once, for no good reason in the world,
it was a plastic gun.
I sat up then. It was nobody's birthday.
Big and black, it was wired to the printed card
that gave its name. *Thompson's Sub.*
He showed me which bit was the magazine.
It was Authentic, the card said.
And he said, too, it's good. Bar size and weight,
the detail's right, exactly like the one
I had.

I yelped thanks and pulled it free
and sprayed the room.

He turned aside and waved a hand before his face.
No. No. Don't point that thing
at me.

Owning

You didn't own much.
No car. No house.
You had some shelves,
some books you buried in the attic
till I dug them out.
Some medals and frayed letters in a drawer.
Some clothes.
Almost, even, a dandy in that,
turning to soft collars late,
bearing in your tie a dandy's pin
a tiger's eye the colour of your own.
I watched you, alien familiar,
as you watched yourself
not taken in.

And I catch myself
in the quality of a sigh
or throwing my weight on one foot
jingling the change in my pocket
failing to not look bored
while the children finish the fairground ride,
I catch myself
looking at the ground, holding my mouth
the way you did.

It's not so much I'm turning into you
but that I was never anybody else.
It was just you had to die and time to turn
for me to shuffle into place.
You knew you never even owned the gestures
that were so completely you.
And while I fell and rose on the passing horse
you never said.

Old

Towards the end
he asked for a mirror.
He sat up in bed
and smoothed the beard from his mouth
judged the sweep of plastic tube
they'd taped across his head into his nose,
and combed and combed his hair.

What's left but habit's vanity
when the rest is gone?

A shuffled twelve yards for a piss
is the centre of the day,
the strain at stool
almost too much to bear.
Even negatives have left.
No evacuation.
No closing of the throat.
Aspiration now's
to drown in spit.
All the racks of language
have been smashed
and thrown out to the dogs.

What is it stares
at the wrecked frames
and tries to guess the gaps?
What stares at the dogs
running in the snow
their slavering mouths
locked on mangled alphabets
it never can make out?

Twyn yr Hyddod

I've had enough of elegies
but must have you know
that mountain where I used to run
marking bounds at the edge of breath,
how its roads exotically wind
among the skirts of hill,
its acres of snapped stone
hard turf and whin
ignore the long slopes' fall
to where the pit no longer is.

His thrown ash has left no scent or mark.
The smell's of nothing but bright air.
And for sound
hear a skylark, who
forgetting she's a cliché
always on the brink of falling, climbs
singing up through daylight
just far enough to break your heart.

Look

In the nightmare
a door of the wardrobe
in childhood's bedroom opens
on its own.

Familiar scrapings in the hinge.
The rack of headless coats.
And fixed inside the door,
the long mirror
in its silvered mounts
has been waiting
all this time.

The dark's slow
in leaving it,
thins like cloudshadow
as it turns its face
to me.

And when I step into
its line of sight,
there's the other man
who's stepped out
of the hanging coat

pale and overweight
and self possessed
and not my self.

Aubade in middle age

The inchlong vapour trail dissolves
fast as the blind invisible head of jet
scores sky
– a dead slow meteor or a speeded comet –
gives in its vanishing tail a sliver of the sun
that hasn't risen yet
on your icestiff patch of earth.

Anaemic rim of fading moon
lets go at last
and vanishes.
Steel Venus rising
falls back to the colour of the sky.
That colour that you couldn't name
resolves to taut thrush egg.
Rags of cloud come
hard as gunmetal.

And you resume yourself
with the ache of gravity
and the strangeness of a leaving dream.
Whatever it was
has dropped you here
and gone.

Day after day
sense and daylight crowd the window
to haul you back and then resculpt the world
with muscular volume, shade and weight,
to whisper again the old advice:
Come on. Wake up. Time to try again.
Time to seal the meat,
to set the day's pot cooking.

Meilyr's song

River rolling on the plain.
A harvest full and certain.
Mountain sprawling pass and ban
can give a glimpse of heaven.
Farmer tending to his herd.
Ten thousand years remembered.

River rolling on the plain.
A compass for a captain.
Mountain sprawling pass and scree.
An outpost for a sentry.
Fields on fire, running men.
The butchered lie forgotten.

Photograph of Captain Oates

You think of James Robertson Justice
– it wasn't him but you know what I mean –
booming, perfecting a one-trick act
before he walks across the blizzarding
screen that will morph into a career
of finding vehicles to boom in.
Meanwhile
John Mills looks worried again!
Sir Lancelot Spratt
On Ice!
Think Vaughan Williams. Think Slimbridge.

But this.
Some bloke
hair thick and cropped
dirty sweater looking itchy.
A bit knackered. Probably
got a roll-up smouldering
out of shot.
Older brother might have been in punk band.

And he's at the end
of growing out of things.
All this, for instance.
Steel needles in his pissedoff eyes
say: Sod this for a game of frozen soldiers.
And you can fuck off for a start.

Occupied

Shy Ghurkas walking from the camp
smile at my children,
like to say hello.

The young Scot who lives across the road
drinks cans of lager in his livingroom
and, out of battledress,
wears shorts patterned with a union jack.

Doveflutter deepened on an endless loop
is helicopters
some bulbeyed and filmy
others heavy, hung on glimmering blades,
gundecks slung over Usk,
pinched up at either end
like a canoe.
They name them after beaten people.

Apache. Iroquois. Chinook.

Toy revolver

He loves its pointed symmetry
the lazy, opened hook of trigger
stock shaped to the palm
like a lover's hip,
opens it like unstoppering a flask
of magic that might spill.

He holds the chamber,
sectioned like fruit, close
to see each scoop and groove
each empty socket in the disc,
counts with a fingertip
six spaces for the dark seeds.

The astronomer's daughter

As the earth turned
the Astronomer Royal
wearing his hat and gown
climbed his tower after the sun had set
to count unreachable stars.
And they were seven sisters
trailed from a rim of moon.

But she did not look up,
gazed, rather, back into the room
shrunk too tiny for her older self
with all its shine and comfort –
the dark furs and the jewelled toys –
which would when that moon
waxed to blood
become invisible,
go out of reach.

the very temple

and troubled we drove from A Toxa
up through Galicia and through Asturias

under the huge Picos
and by ship ploughed north

through pale glitter of the rough Atlantic
and a crewman pointed and called

et lá les dauphins
and perhaps I did or didn't catch

their dark rims arching through the dazzle
breaching ocean nosing north with us

like a sign of the dark miracle
and in our heads a line grew on a map

like a graphic in a fifties film
and among the onboard trashy shop stuff

they sold the dark specs in cardboard frames
and at the dock the young crew even wore them

lined the deck and looked up for the unshow
and leaving them we drove again

and the nosing mapline of our road east
lay in the exact track of it

and *here* I said *it's nearly time*
and found a quiet lane under a brow of hill

and people were climbing there to watch
and we waited with the car pulled to the hedge

the cooling metal ticking
and there was cloud like smoky glass across his face

when out of the west a bead a bud
of darkness hardened in the air

and grew and pushed a dark beam overland
a dark plough over fields and hills

and we could see the width the north and south
of it and through a thinning of the cloud

the pale sun ghosted
and the bud grew broad and sped

rushed like the ground when you fall
and at once and slowly

invisible moon bit at the rim of the sun
or slid her wafer onto his seared white tongue

and the bud was as broad as the land
and it swallowed the hill and the hedge

and it swallowed the watchers and car
and cold poured over us

and nature was struck dumb
just like the papers said

and in the very temple of totality
she called his name

and there was the flash and click
that should have broken something

but did not
and there was discovered smiling

his face as pale as planets strong and hurt
our twelve years' son

the only thing there was in all that dark
and the timerush regathered

and the sun breached from shadow
discovering the ordinary

as the stone of the moon rolled away
and birds stirred and the world warmed

Seaward

I've ridden out
on the gull's back
and snapped out patterns
from the glittering track
of going sun

and all that riding
all that patterning
has no more sense
no more significance
nor any greater thing
than's in the ineluctable
present tense.

Seven cities

My son on Castell Dinas

Later, we walked up to the dinas holding hands.
Fosse, tump and cliff, erupted meeting place
of limestone and red sand,
grass sheepshitten and sheepcropped,
hawthorn and decaying fences.
Eastward, the track along the ridge
and all its folds of mountain falling north.
Westward, Mynydd Troed across the bwlch
hard and darkening in late afternoon.

The Cessna towed a glider overhead
snorting in laborious air.
Its shadow rippled on the pant
and the gravel droning died.

Released, he ran and played and made discoveries
and cairns and cromlechs
from the shale of fallen towers.

I saw grass and earth and stone
lichened, split, layered like the name –
castell – men in helmets holding natives down,
dinas – city before Rome breathed.
Cattle, slaves and iron bars.

A mile of air fell down towards the farms
blurring smoky in the shade.
Above the cup of land and ring of scarp,
high, the glider's lazy tilt and wheel
caught late sun on the wings,
glass teardrop of cockpit gleaming
pearly as aluminium.

He rampaged on the parapets,
slipped from my reaching hand
cartooned to thirty yards of shadow.

I watched the ridge of Mynydd Troed turn black,
the Cessna dropping in to shadow
trailing rope.

Siesta time in the Labyrinth

Cypresses like gloomy flames
motionless along the hills
echo the stone horns round the parapets
still as the hot oils in the pithoi
under the heatstruck slabs
or as the loose knots of the royal snakes
silent in their pit
too baked to find their own heads in the coils.

The snake goddess has taken the day off.
Her clay breasts itch with heat
but she sits with outstretched dusty arms
not bothering to scratch
and, almost, sleeps.

Around the inner courtyards
young men lie naked in thin strips of shade.
Their blades and doubleheaded axes
photograph the glare,
too fixed to glint.

And in the reek of his dark stall,
his slobber barely troubling to ooze,
the sculpted bull
enacts a kind of standing death.

They can't think
to dance across his back
to slit his throat and venerate his blood.
Not today.

Passageways and landings, halls
encase squat blocks of standing air
gone thick with heat.
Down a folded, angular wide stair
beside a square pool ironed flat,

the clay reports of his ministers untouched,
the king in a dirty singlet
lies on his couch
and sweats.

The only god this afternoon
is the sun.
Every day he comes like this
and clamps them
squeezes life down to a thread
that, almost, snaps
in cypress, snake and goddess
and man and bull and king.
And then he eases loose his grip
and lets them wake.
Because it will not be today.
Not yet.

Gothic

do you see these meteors? do you behold these exhalations?

You've stepped into the unlit kitchen
where one gasjet flares

pulsing its splayed coronet on dark.
The hot attenuated lilac

sheathes each furious steady lancet tongue
of petrol blue.

The lovely lit transparency
hangs upside down in air

some luminous horror
swimming below the thermocline

hellchoir flung back
gaping in oblation

hissing, somehow, the Japanese for
yes.

*

Or
you've seen the documentaries.

In the deepest places of the sea
blowholes spurt volcanic pus.

After the million quiet acres
your camera comes to them

where plates grind and magma
growing lips and spitting

fantasticates the seam
with burning stacks and bubbling towers

tumbling lava and wet smoke
up into the dark.

And this boil of sudden energy
breeds blind unthinkable citizens.

*

Or after the wide worked carpet
of the dark Atlantic breathing

thirty thousand feet below
you've left the dark streettongues

the trashlovely shops around the base
and with the crowds come through

the foyer's marbled mausoleum
polished to an art deco binge

up through the stacked floors
to this midnight platform

to see the deep symmetric seams
break open hot with taillights

to see night carved in blocks and spires
by the slots of lighted rooms

rivers notated by absence
copters marked by juddering lights

swimming above to watch the spectacle
and be it.

This high and at minus eight
the city whiffs of burger fat and burning gas

 and you're braided in the fuse
feeling the cold of its controlled burn

where all the gabbled syllables
distill to that harsh aspirant

hhhhhhhhhhhhhhhhhhhh
ye-air-sss.

The planet's venting into space
sucking strength like fire

through its roots
to blow it into dark

blowtorching you transparent
to one more tongue that screams delight

in that thrilled uprush
of its own annihilation.

.el ad cit His breach ,en heav
us and ou r mouth imp ugn

in y it un and tion ec Perf
Then my unc le said, the sense is this.

(.come would les ab syll no mo ly On)
the myth we live in makes no sense.

,said brother My .breathe to hard got It
the stone way up and make the gate of god.

wind to cupola on road and
for him, paving track on arch

fly stone make to on trod and
chisel men. We shook our heads

fawning on nodding ,bluff the on ermined
towards god. I saw him once, Nimrod,

tower Nimrod's tonguing ,work the of
of fired slime along each terrace

bricks the and ashlar the lift to
and I trod in the drum thirty years

mill the and windlass the worked
For three hundred years my family

erthe the all of lippe the confounded was there for

Builders of Bab-ilu

                    b   a   b a ba barbar bar bar bare
Unc looked up at no thing and gasped

            .ar Shin on bet a alph an rain and hail
fell. We watched him at om ize to

            ,fell he and out slide foot er's broth
the   the   Meis sel. And I saw my

                    ,cŷn the, ta talt the no, said le
Still, hand me the scalp rum my unc

            .loose work nouns the all and ash to
I saw the pre po sit ions flake

            up ing look but wau en of full fa ber a
to work. Hand me the   my unc said. I wheeled

            tried we Still .void of cold but wrath of
tar word to word. We shook. Not heat

            mor not could You .cuit bis as ble
hard as mou ntain ice, went fri a

            froze bricks slime The .fall to man ing
wax won't melt, but freeze for the fly

            high This .thin grow sky the saw and
I looked up at the fur ther works

            floor enth sev and dred hun nine sand
spoke. And as we worked on the thou

            he as ered shiv he But .heat His
No good can come and we will feel

Europe after the rain

After Max Ernst

Keep down. The cellar's safer.
The precincts and the tenements
are skewed and buckled
the stacked floors frozen in mid slither.
Melted glass and steel
Have iced and blistered into flesh.
But over there, look,
Among the standing girders' green and dun
the giant madman in the zany's hat
and the statuebird
shut wings locked like armour on her flanks
watch and watch whatever there is
beyond them in the square

where a magus saw the stars revolve
where Wales was set upon a spike to rot
where Vesalius flayed the puppet man
where the French sword severed
the adulterous queen's head
where Regiomontanus tried to set his clock
to which trams ran to time
on which the tired clerk rode home
thinking of light
where we saw Tendulkar's running one hand catch
where ja outside the Rathaus
Magdeburg's horses trying to tear apart an idea
ripped their sinews
where somebody nailed a big list to a door
where the Popoli burned the Nobili's golden book
where the old god waved to the crowd
and death waved back
where authors combed their manes
and gave up roaring
where l'Empereur set up an obelisk
where they built and then tore down a wall
where the cleanshaven

smashed the shops of the bearded
where victors waved from armoured cars
where Monique slit her Klaus's throat
pour la patrie
where every year drunks danced in fountains
where they released the doves and the balloons
where they unveiled the great monument
where once a year the great stood silent
where gulls and pigeons limed
old murderers' bronze heads
where the Archduke learnt how soft he was
and gasped

the madman and the statue stare
at the blackened flags,
the scattered bits, the empty space

and nothing has ever been so still
as this:
the figures that could be bits of wall
the blistered walls that could be live
and puncturing the fret of green and rust
the poison rinse of chlorine sky
without a wing alive in it
without a wing alive.

Rat

The last city
rots in the gutter
eyes milky and viscous.
The snout's hard back. Paws clench
on nothing.
In the collapsed abdomen
a million citizens are busy.

Sailing past Antipolis

After Picasso

Come with me to the rail and look
oh look –

that woman
with the flailing hair
the breasts that swing.
What clefts and curves
what skipping feet,
the lofted planet of her tambourine!
Her kids all dance
and the band, too, 's hoofing.

The far off tune's as crisp as wine
I know the key.
The piper sitting
a shade apart
blowing his notes into bright blue air –
he could be me.

And all the rooftops
and the sands
the mountains singing the same blue song
the moving figures and the woman too
slide leftwards, dancing, out of frame
and past.
Outside the town where the song goes small
the green woods breathe.

I think I might have lived
in this town once.

Acknowledgements and notes

Some poems have previously appeared in *Annetna Nepo, New Orleans Review, New Welsh Review, Plamak, Planet, Poetry London, Poetry Wales, Quattrocento, Research Matters* (University of Glamorgan) and the anthologies, *Poetry in the Parks* edited by Wendy Bardsley (Sigma) and *Wading Through Deep Water* edited by Tony Curtis (Coychurch Press).

A version of 'Meilyr's song' was first published in dismembered form scattered in the prose of my novel *Griffri*. 'Life of the Poet (index)' draws together and adapts material from the indices of several literary biographies. 'Sailing past Antipolis' is based on Picasso's 1946 painting 'Joie de Vivre'. Picasso wrote the word 'Antipolis' ('the city opposite') on the back of the canvas.